PSALMODY

WINNER

OF

THE

MELITA

HUME

POETRY

PRIZE

2015

MARIA APICHELLA
Psalmody

EYEWEAR PUBLISHING

First published in 2016
by Eyewear Publishing Ltd
Suite 333, 19-21 Crawford Street
Marylebone, London W1H 1PJ
United Kingdom

Cover design and typeset by Edwin Smet
Author photograph by Caroline Apichella, cfaapichella.com
Printed in England by TJ International Ltd, Padstow, Cornwall

*Eyewear wishes to thank Jonathan Wonham for his
generous patronage of our press.*

WWW.EYEWEARPUBLISHING.COM

Dedicated to
Andrea Pirovano

THE
MELITA HUME
POETRY PRIZE

Maria Apichella is a 2015 winner of the Melita Hume Poetry Prize.
She received £750 and this publication by Eyewear Publishing.
The 2015 Judge was Toby Martinez de las Rivas.
His citation read:

Above and beyond the technical skill on display in each poem,
what I most admired in this collection was its searingly intelligent
intimacy, a deeply constructed symbolism which constantly resurfaces
throughout the book, and a powerful, direct, unsettling,
and at times very beautiful and stark lyricism.

Maria Apichella
completed her PhD in English
and Creative Writing at The University of
Aberystwyth in Wales. She now teaches with
the University of Maryland, University College,
Europe. Her pamphlet *Paga* was a winner
of the Cinnamon Press Pamphlet
competition 2014. This is
her first collection.

TABLE OF CONTENTS

1.

Friday traffic to Bala
through mizzle, alone,
psalms whispering like a cassette.

The moon criss-
crossing the A
497, revelation of hills
like a face shimmering in a dark car.

Gravel prattles. I've arrived. The honey
cakes hot in Tupperware; apple, cinnamon
imbues. I'm tired; jangled, I carry a box
of many flavoured choices.

Friends of other friends roil, the front
door ajar, smokers silhouetted like saints,
arms wide, palms open. 'Come
in, and know us better.'

The beat of the evening is underway. A couple
neck in the corner, a man in thick
glasses chews the crackling. Crystal
glasses scattered like puddles, filled
or spilled, maroon wine, ochre beer alight
under candle and lamp. Cakes left in the hubble-
bubble kitchen, so many faces half-recognised
from the Arts Centre, *Tree House*, Barclays,
the Bus Stop.

A man laughs; a ring-
leader on leave.
He's strumming on a stool.

'Sing for us, David,'

someone calls.

2.

Corn-stubble face
looking at me
curious.

A full presence –

like the song he sings
expansive as tributaries

makes me shell   target   bird.

3.

David approached,

damp from singing, ruddy
from cycling steep,
twisty B-roads
from New Cross. Tanned legs bristled
with muddy miles. 'Wales is beautiful,'
he said, '*so* beautiful.'

Later he was lost; too tipsy to find his room,
everyone sacked on sofas, floors – laughing,
the leader in blue
cycling shorts
pacing
the shadowy corridor like a porter.

4.

Saturday morning, he came down clean,
ate the honey cakes cold.

Later, something he said —
taking his regiment to Rome,
never following recipes,

made me weightless. I walked
slow-mo for hours,
                          cartwheeled.

5.

That morning
he knocked a jar over.
Toast-flecked honey inched
across the breakfast table
like dense sunlight;
anyone else would have scooped it back in,
ashamed to waste
in a gnawed up world.
Yet he let it spill,
washed out the jar
poured in new amber

a slow coming sweetness,
                    a kiss.

6.

He likes coffee
strong,
was immersed in explaining
how a sheep is shorn.
Scrutinized that tea-stained map
of Ceredigion on the wall in the kitchen:
this place my home
land   inheritance. Standing
on the table to make his point.

Blushed when he choked
on his steaming brew;
eats basil-green pesto by the spoon,
loves big farm-house yards, mud.

He fires questions like a fairground gun –
often missing the target.

7.

David dances like a man alone.
David sings disaster.
David's all blush
chisel
copper
grizzle
thick
bone.

8.

So he can sing and dance?
He is a Welshman after all.

He's leaving for the desert.
Just *imagine* what could happen,
          God forbid.
I'd be crushed as road kill.
I cannot help but question:
Does he know the Lord?
…
So what's his life about?
I want to know.

Forget this David.

You had a one night's *chat?*
He won't remember you for that.

9.

We walk. He's all
kindness, green, corduroy brown.

I am frenetic
blue; tension under a cool-headed guise.

I speak in slow bursts.
He keeps me going
with questions like a good teacher;
speculative, always
sketching pictures with his talk.

Here he is now, trudging
the ruffled Llyn Tegid;
skies pour to the silky tangle
rocky land and lake.

He points out birds hovering low,
names them, translating Welsh
words for my English mouth:
Bwncath   *hawk.*
I can't imagine his thriving
in flatlands, sand, thudding heat.

Can't see him cradling
a rifle, letting it rest
in his arms, waiting
for his clattering chest to slow,
his breathing steady. David
shrunk to the function of a gun.

Who wants an absent partner, tense
with tooth-breaking secrets, whose body is
owned by government men?
Whose job's all jargon, bullet-
holed paper work.
Who plans to occupy, re-make cities,
countries, traditions, bedrooms.

I'd always be listening to the radio.
I can't be stoic.
How can he share the dirt of his life?
The tunnels, maps, diversions.
He is bound by laws – as I am.
Love's the law I obey.
I should forget him.
His mud,
          his heavy bones.

10.

I'm a Monastery carved into a granite hill.
From my stone shelter I gaze on the brown-stained valley
I've chosen. I've conquered Cymru, the lippy coast
of Ceredigion is mine; Aberystwyth the adopted harbour
of my homecoming. My ancestors were priests in Naples.
Like them I read and spin a house of sacred words.
I grow tomatoes in terracotta pots, sweet yellow peppers.
I keep tadpoles, make my toothpaste from baking soda.
I'm chirpy with the elderly neighbors; pay my rent on time,
keep the radio a quiet hymn at night. I need nothing but silence,
a room, billowy white and airy, friends living in the scenery.
My back's turned from the nightly hubbub of bars,
my face examines the cobblestones. The psalms bubble
with words free from context, emptied of time and place,
as I wish to be.

Yet the market farmers know my name.
I've become that funny-faced woman setting
up camp in this damp, salty town of bonfire parties.
I'm a twig of light blown from the beach.
I'll not return to the source, annihilated, ridiculous
by Eros.

11.

Who is this man? An atheist, un-
shaven soldier.
Priest-like in stillness, sun-
like in presence sitting
opposite me, knee against knee,
talking   on and on.

12.

'I'm a cartographer,' he says.
'Land reader, paper-pusher.
More than a recruit.

I'm like King David
the virile, weepy bard.
Didn't he say it's not *good* to be alone?

Or was that Jehovah Jireh
whose grace is sufficient for thee?'

He remembers that phrase from Sunday school.
'That and my cousin Carys stripping
off her pink lace frock, screaming
in naked circles about the altar like a banshee.'

Is nothing sacred? I ask.
                        'Yes.
        The force that through the green
        fuse drives the flower;

Stony one. You are
no monastery.
They are full of men,
mutts, beggars.
If you are,
you must let me in.
I am all these and more.'

13.

I'm thirsty as earth in high summer.

14.

Last night in the low-
beamed dark I dreamt David

was blind,
foaming
into my room roaring
like the break
of a pent gorge. I wrestled
him out. His rugby boy-
boned weight   the pummelling
arms of my fear.

I wake   recognize I've taken a wrong
turning; thirsted
for a doubter –
a man not
my kind.
I'm leaving, unquenched as a bird pecking
on ice. I deny
this. I need no one.

All loyalty but the numinous
fails.
Like King David,
I trust the invisible.
I will not stumble at beauty, as he did,
glancing at skin I can't
touch. I take the empty roads,
arc round bald mountains. The steep
drops close
to the spinning wheels,
the dim light, my road, visible   for now.

15.

Shabbat's for the faithful. It's melting
for September. I walk
the dusky prom. Freshers flit; a smog
of human bees. The town buds and flourishes
with boys,
girls taut with summer
still warm on their bellies who live
& move & have their kicks
as a team of moving nerves legs   lost keys.
They live in a nearby hive. Sleep in pockets behind sticky
walls of sound.
Waxed up each dusk they do
the ecstatic Waggle to the Union, the Pier, back
to base. I glance from behind glass,
        this frisson, this time of making mead.
I've outlived their cycle, the three-year generation.
I'm sealed; permanent as Constitution Hill.
I'll stay till I have scratched
all my itchy questions.

16.

Spirit of illumination,
where are you on a Saturday night?
Do I need to woo you
with candles? Why do the cynical thrive?
I've flung down my life like a Turkish rug.
When will you bring me
home to your shelter? Let me breakfast in wheat-
flaked gratitude. Let all my feelings be simple,
painless to share like cigarettes, salt, directions to *The Black
Lion*. Let grace pad out my life like green sodden grass. Protect
me from loving accidentally, slipping on the wet shingle,
lurching into the tide   desiring,
drowning. If you will not answer,
bandage me in blankets   of weakness strongly.

17.

David unearthed me, fidgeting
between pages, cold mugs of Darjeeling.
How did you *find* me?
          I lifted my eyes up to the hills.

Ever the soldier, sheep farmer's son,
hunted me like I'd hoped,
herding me into the sun,
asking, 'how do you spend your days?'

Chewing the psalms of David.

He asks: 'Why those pious songs
when there's jazz?'

★

Because I sense webbed dimensions.
A being ingenious beyond my ken;

when I frame God, he blasts outward,
glints catching in all places.

★

Agape – bedrock beneath cathedrals, how do I respond?

I've met another who fathoms me; not afraid, uninterested
or taken. He knows I come with you attached.

18.

Agape,
you are the anchor
I cannot lose.

You are not
a gold-cheeked
icon, a marble statue
sunk below gloom, known
only by fish and divers.

Hidden one, enter
the beat of this day.

Don't be civil,
waiting to be noticed
like a Verger at a fete, awkward
in collared cassock.

          Announce your arrival
                 like hail.

19.

Blessed are they who are picky
with friends; who turn people like peaches
in the hot slant of a fly-flicked market.

They are a flask of chilled water, poured
into empty cups. A bowl of washed apples
next to puffs of pink candy floss.
A stone in our shoe, slowing us down,
a splinter of mirrors, our view.

What is this word,
'Blessed'?
a word I finger about, thick segments
of oranges
arranged on a blue plate.
I spit sour flesh, pips for the juice,
chewable drinkable sun.

Who are these *wicked*
I must avoid to be *blessed*?

Is David wicked? Am *I* blessed?

Father, you are made of passion
in all its bitter green flavours.
This I've known from childhood.
You make and re-make all things
willing to be touched.
Do not make me reduce my heart
eyes, thoughts to *us*   *them.*

I know no assassins in this corner of Wales.
I have done no serious harm with these hands.
Yet in my mind I have
denied
cheated
stultified.

20.

David, I've gone
and poured stewed tea. We've talked
too long, already –

Oregano,
how best to sauté mushrooms.

You don't
dwell on the invisible, you eat
your mushrooms raw.

Doubt dissolved
when I was seven, in an August heat,
perching on an iron fence,
tonguing chocolate ice-cream.

I like Portobello mushrooms browned
over beach coals, onions scorched red;
Lidl's finest feta, cracked pepper, black.

The tickle of smoke, salt, grainy sand.
The flushed evening
melts into the sea,
fades to a duck egg dawn.

Before you leave
I've made you a clove-studded orange.
Breathe cinnamon,
citrus,
morning air
                    a gift.

21.

'I'm both bull and lamb,'
David says.
'Not good,
not wicked –
          like you.
Our longings pattern parallel lines.
Don't enclose me in your boxed-up words,'

he's right (about so many things.
More clear and kind than I)
and yet he says:

'I do not fear what I cannot see.
I trust in bodies, minds, soil.
Why should I twist to spirits?

Why?'

22.

David's a good man, soothing
as tea, strong as a leather arm
chair, tenderly rational,
he makes your name a litany
of by-words when he trips
on concrete, slops milky oatmeal
on the floor, or at a joke I tell
badly. I do not tut. I'm not sour,
a record-keeping nun.
He won't be defined   just loved.
We will be parted   what then?

Who is he in darkness?

                    Who am I at dawn?

23.

Be wise, be warned! The Prime Mover
is colossal, a throne-sitting chess player.
Massive in form   in promise,
he calls for discussion   I'm calling for inspiration,
a psalmody with David
a singing fighter, for God says: 'Ask of me and I will give.'

David doesn't hear a thing, yet I say
yes   I *shall* ask for miracles —

healings / epiphanies / conversion
transcendence / keys to be found
October's rent / bullets to dodge.

Why not live with expectation?
Create in us a triangulation.
Doesn't a unity of three strings
make a cord less easy to fray?
Yet David won't be looped.
He keeps snapping
          my ropey psalms.

24.

Yes, body is good. And you,
frank as a child, freckled
together, standing close, almost
oblivious
are good as bread,
summer
light.

Your skin, wind-tanned, warm
near mine
awkward   ecstatic   hope.

You're clean glass;
a reflection tested
with my fingertips, my faith
that body is good.

25.

From birth I was cast
upon God. I was born
hungry. I never had enough. I was named
after resilient widows:
         Marie   Betty   Louise.
I carried them like apple-seeds
of hermit tendencies. Today I could
correct my curled up past. Be chosen
un-cry the weeping
baby I was. My lonely
room is cramped as the womb.
No more do I want
to be called
Abandoned, Sad; One who was Forgot.
I want to burn
the sick seeds. Start again.
Father, feed me now, re-
name me.
Let it be you
who carves the good promises
on the trunk of my body.
Make my name a synonym
for Beulah.

26.

You're back,
David,
like grease in hair.

        Grey crescent,
        dirt under nails.
        Either I'm too much ahead
or you're too far behind. Even in sleep snippets
loom and snipe, for the dips and sidling shadows in your skin
are like mine.

This week I've called to heaven.   *You've* replied,
pooling into my thoughts, the same old jokes & spiels.
You set my groceries on the floor with a bang,
tell the same stories
the same tone,
always an untidy truth.

You are like fingers after chopping chillies,
burning deeply long.
You soak down to the thud
and pith of me till all my blood
rings at the sound of your laugh.

27.

David calls   I'm ignoring him   No,
I'm answering   leaving this shaded cloister.

I throw open the doors. David's camping beyond
the boundaries, teasing on the horizon's
edge.
'Don't
be afraid of the dark,' he says.
'Where you are going I have gone.'

The night is present. It rubs
against me like a cat.
Drizzle, little slaps of wind. The stars spit
on this steep slip-shod road. How long
have I edged through pockets of closed fields?
Past silhouettes of cautious sheep.

I fear the groan of mother-cows
– the shock
of sudden crows, rising.
A mosquito worries close,
bites of doubt appear.
So much could go wrong with the moon
on the move, these dark sky tricks
the sudden curve of cliffs and
should I be here?

I am on the way. Galumphing
towards my Love in walking boots,
smelling like puddles, salt. The night
smeared across my face.

Hitch me
to him like a caravan to a bumper.
I am coming
stupidly as the stars.

28.

Today the turquoise view
swoops faster, swirls like lime juice in a cold glass,
the bay flashes, tumescent, a noon-time joy, steep to the side.
The early moon a pale slice in blue. Scent of manure and hay blow,
sheep wink, coastline trees like brown twiggy hair blowing sideways.
My David's a pebble of strength too bright,
too smooth to be flung.
Nothing's certain but changing landmarks, sifting coves.
We're aware of each other's breathing; the Mini's forced nearness,
the sun catching his knuckles, freckled wrist, silver watch,
his quiet shifting of the gears, dusty brown Topsiders stepping hard
on the gas   rising   high.
And down
                deep to the mossy,
                valley house. A white block
                windowed memory.
We click still.
A net curtain moves.

Before I meet his mother
he takes me
among his father's rocky fields,
shows me how to swindle
honey from a hive.
With a cigarette '*just for this purpose*'
he puffed acrid smoke like an old rusty engine.
A slow thrum,
the sound of tiny drills.
The conquered *Gwenynen Fêl*
shot up, away into the blue,
her drones chasing like a chorus of boy-lovers.
I had been hungry.
He gave me the first sticky comb.

29.

I'm nothing like David's mother. Not chic,
hosting dinners for *y bonedd*, serving little tipples, smoked
salmon canapés. I've one pair of real leather shoes;
the rest are from charity shops.

My father paints canvases but they're obnoxious; vast
too big for walls, they spread
red haze, rock-blue,
granite lipped. I am like him,
seeing rocks as springs.
The mountains dissolving
into red, white, pink wine set at our table.
We drink all to the dregs and gravel.
I've loved wrongly, rightly;
been struck by lightning once
again. The electricity
of these furious devotions

expands me.

30.

I can only give thanks for Adoni is good as a watermelon on a hot day.
You will find me chewing psalms like pink mesocarp pulp spitting sticky lyrics
that swell beneath consciousness, awareness of the presence of summer,
darting flies, the resting presence of the comforter. A slab of sunlight straddles
my back, dazzles my eyes as David comes near, balancing the take-out coffees,
burning his knuckles. A bucket of ice; yoke-yellow heat. This's no mirage;
I've fallen heavy into the salty river of Adoni's explicit words, explored
along the dusty boundaries, year after year – I've grown into trust
as a face softens with age.
You who have no accent speak every dialect,
play-language between pairs, sisters, friends.
   Agape, Eros.

31.

Lost,
in evening shade,
stretched maple light,
            a *hush* & r u s t l e,
I stand between shelves, searching red,
olive, denim spines
for a book to guide mine like a current,
catching, pulling a catamaran to a chopped up sea.
Titles glance: 'Desire
in Language,' gold of 'intertextuality'
catch like coins in a stream.
            Why do I struggle to understand?
Can I pray for a deeper intelligence?

David would say no.

Like a weaned child is my mind
within me.

Six O'Clock again   I thank you
for the butternut
squash soup
we share from a flask
on the bench,
coffee sweetened with milk.
For David,
this seagulled crying air.

32.

If with your throat,
fingers,
bowels,
you choose to follow fully, blessings
will sprout
like Queen Anne's lace; escort you as scent;
blackberries, Welsh rain,
stone. You'll be blessed in Aberystwyth,
in the bathroom.
The lyrics on your screen, the extension of your mind,
every page of every hardback you skim
– all your friends, your flat pack desk, keys,
green lamp will be hallowed
when you sleep, rise, and on
it goes.

If with your throat,
fingers,
bowels,
you choose to play
games with Yahweh, cherry-
picking principles, curses
like athlete's foot will spread from your soles.
You will be tormented in Aberystwyth,
in the bathroom. The language
on your screen,
the procedure of your mind, every page of every book
you absorb – all your people, your desk, keys,
your green lamp will be troubled.
You will be cursed when you start,
when you finish.

       David cocks his eyebrow.
                   'So primitive.'

33.

Bless me, please. Curses
are little weights and I'm heavy enough.

Tip blessings on me when I'm outside.
Throw them at me when I arrive
at the door. Slip them in my tea
when we meet. Stir them into my words.

Dunk me in pools of blessing, stuff me
like olives. Rub them into the skin
of my hands. Multiply within my life
like cells in my bones. Let them rise
before me like fog, grow under my feet,

shoot back at me when I sneeze.

34.

I do not
experience *Agape*
as a splash
of old water in the eyes,
or as a thick red curtain.
You are not
a sneeze of clover,
the marble weight of beads.

I do not experience you.
I put myself within

your light, your shade.

I do not name you,
do not arrange
your qualities like roses in a vase.
I cannot describe you
like a line of autumn light.

Through clemency
you meet me.

You fill all that can be filled.

35.

We live life to life
like a cloud of tadpoles
swirling in an invisible jar.

God is lidless
filled with drinkable rain,
the shape and dimension
of our days. I sense this.

You don't.
Even so,
we move in the same water
searching our mouth-like brains
for something deep to grow in.

Give me patience.
Contain me —

I am swarming.

36.

I have shelves of Hebrew
poetry David's not
planning to read. All
holy verse was spoilt
for him at school.

The guitar's his delight.
He sings at the basil,
the red geraniums.

37.

David is a wife; roasts chicken
for a saffron paella as I study.
He fixes the tap, makes espresso,
small adjustments around my sphere.

He plays me
jazz; my records,
he says, are tuneless,
too serious.
The Protecting Veil.
Music like our life, a disorder
of strings below the cello
weaving a melody
I can't stop humming.

38.

This one's a protest.

Devotion's a drain; an emptying journey.
David's a rowboat on shadowy breakers.

He's a wreck. Filled with slits,
slats   unfixable
                                  pits
precious as breath.

He takes my weight for now,

lets me burrow in his scoop;
takes me into dark constellations
my pleas
my heat

a white flare in the night.

*

You don't
mean to stir me up.
You don't
know how your touch
triggered a quest into your mind
(freshly broken bread)
your body (ruddy
as high summer)
your open-palmed life. The terrible
fact of death ahead & all the past

drives me
onward.
I'm mapless.

You're lost.

39.

We eat the chicken, somewhat late.

A simmering recipe,   slow
with salted butter &   red wine. An evening
          long as a phone call   I can't afford.

We lean across the table's raft.

40.

David says: Am I not worth more than ten Gods?
Look, these hairy hands hold yours, my coffee
breath may not have created seas, but my voice
is not imagined. My weight pitted against yours
is warm. Here I am, now. I will try to understand,
soften to become strong. Spirits remain obtuse.
I make you howl.
Does Jesus lug your shopping?
Introduce you to Miles Davis' *Blue*
in Green? Chop the white onions so your eyes
don't stream? Does the Holy Spirit banter?
Test out new jokes?
God hammers laws in stone
leaves you to kick.

41.

I dreamt
I dreamt
my light was David's dark.
I spent the night guiding
him across a motorway;
a blind man,
gripping my wrist, shouting questions
as lorries swerved and honked,
their long lights
a torches' dazzle:

> *Tell me, where can I go to learn about God? Who should I speak with?*
> *A Priest, a Jew or you? What time of day is best? Do I rise at dawn,*
> *walk by the sea at dusk – how about my lunch breaks? Does meditating*
> *work if you're Western? If you work ungodly shifts? Why can't the Bible*
> *be a manual, a systematic list? Do's, don'ts's would be easier than this*
> *doorstop of a book. All the transmuted poetry, patriarchal history,*
> *love-making in meadows, tent peg deaths, scatter-gun descriptions,*
> *sacred boxes, floating zoos, a compendium of antiphonal voices:*
> *are they still relevant? Why? Why am I cursed with these eyes?*

I woke exhausted. My belief, his un-
belief. My habit is not his. Why
do we share this daily draw?
I hope in an unseen force. I call
to God, asking: 'Open
wide David's sealed windows;
blow in as light, speak as this sea-spray
softly within his ear-muffled silence.
Let there be a man meeting man,
a holy maleness I cannot construct.

42.

By day the Lord directs his love,
at night his tune is with me –

he pours
water into a glass bowl.
        He leans askance.
Wakes me under rushing taps
                of light.

At noontime, he slopes in un-
seen
at the high window.
A big face filled with jokes & pain.

He washes the lunchtime hustle;
school-aged bullies & adult victims;

manipulators, saints & seekers &
finders: those who cut skin, ties,
all contact
        and me.
Another in the barrage
of bodies protected, unaware,
under blocks of yellow.
He winked,   re-filled the bowl
behind my eyes
for a moment,
            weightless.

43.

I don't
understand how well we work.
You, the narrow-
minded atheist,
(as I once called you) I, the holy-
roller
                    (as you like to say).
What have we ever discussed, what did we ever do,
which was not infected by the Invisible
(as you call it)?
Devotion's embodied like stitches in the reasons
I've given for everything you've asked:

   'Why will you kiss me but not finish the job?
   Why are you antsy about Yoga?
   What's wrong with pinching a few packets of paper from the office?'

My faith with its ebbs   a river refusing to dry.
David, you are a miracle   a force I can't encompass.
You chose me   I belong to you, or I want to
loosely.
You are all red-tongued opinion. I love to argue back,
Celtic talker, poet-mouth; you never stop exploring,
taking everything apart like a nerd. Your decisions
are as concrete. Your arrogance disturbs me. You get
in my way; waste time, always offer another outlook.
Yet you open up crazy doors, let me walk (or push me in).
You make me caw like a bird. I'm sick that you cannot
drink with me this good red wine, chew these fresh wheat
rolls. You who reject a reality you call a fantasy;
born in tradition
fostered in habit,
carried by neuroses.
No.

44.

I know the numinous in the cold
morning clatter.

A love submerged
in first thoughts, arising from dreams
as sea-salt, persistent as the alarm.

A love I will keep reaching into,
a perfect paradox like raggedy gulls
settled upon the reel of storm caps

like orange buoys   like bubbles.

45.

We walk the spine of the prom
to church.

Your first time since
school days, already irritated.

Light and tiny wings   touch
the   air that touches us. All around
shit falls.

They say if you're hit you are lucky,
or blessed.
Today, by some joke, you are chosen.
'Why me?' you yell at the heaving sky
as blessings spatter your tweed jacket
like shots of spilt cream.

You think perhaps it's a sign
you're not meant to come.
I scoff, finger-comb your hair,
kiss flutteringly as we shelter
in a doorway.

We arrive late
untidy
at the big wooden door.

46.

At church they sing anthems;
African   beats,
          Welsh hymns.
They call for the King of Glory
to come, to stay as long as he likes,
visit them in their granite town,
resting between the seas cracked lips
on the gritty brink of nowhere,
speak in their accents,
possess them   if He will.
They are servants,
will use their kitchens,
make broth, beans, baked potatoes
for whoever's hungry.
They will write cheques, lend books,
live out their everyday theology.
They see themselves as pots.
Solid, plain, designed to absorb fire,
continual use.

47.

I stand afraid.
What if we all sang in all the anger
sadness
all the truth we know?

★

I'm done with censorship.
If David won't hear me worship
he'll never know the core of me.
He mouths the hymns, twitchy
an out-of-place school boy.

Be Thou my Vision, O Lord of my heart.

I raise my arms.
He sinks to the pew,
coughs at the stone flagged floor.
We're both angry –
don't know why.
I call outward;
believe I'm heard –
yes –
          'by the man in the sky.'

★

Walking home he said
I looked ridiculous.

> *Just keep composed,*
> *don't be so expressive.*

Or later:

> *My mother*
> *goes to chapel*
> *be like her —*
> *keep up an acquaintance with God.*

★

No.

I come to pour out my marrow,
un-skimping, I want to be holy.

I have one life, body a choice
to resist or engage with a God.

If I were bolder I would dance,
use my arms to frame him.

★

David slams the pots, saying
he is angry that he is angry,
frightened by his fear;
the nakedness of my hope.
He says, he's cautious
of the invisible well
I tap into when I pray.
To him I am amphibian —
half body, half spirit,
bird and fish.
He says:
'You raise hell in me.'

I beckon from the inlet
holding a book of stories.
His need of me a blunt fact.
Me and my belief –

'not harmless   not twee.'

★

David, what can I say to make you happy?
I have found –
        No –
I've *been* found.

★

Walking along the prom after dinner
the sea-sucking shingle-sounds soothe
my ringing, sinks the words I've said, heard.
At home I let the hot tap run.
It fogs the mirror, hides my face.
Water needs to scald to cleanse.

Water will take complete possession.
It slides me off my feet,
sweeps beyond the horizon.

David, I say, love
remakes you.
I was revived.
I went into the wide
water as a pickled old woman,
sunk down and died.

I came bubbling up
a baby, bobbing, smiling
alive.

★

David says: 'I don't understand
your watery jargon.
Your guide's a trickster,
a creation in your story-telling mind.
A stick (a phallic image at that)
you hold over your back.'

He says I relish un-
happiness,
thwarting, the taste of guilt.

'Who wants an invisible rival?
A being who takes all joy,
rigging it with conditions.'

★

David,
we speak a separate language
even affection
even desire
even we
          cannot gloze.

48.

For years I let a raven
make my shoulders a perch,
his beak over my head
the peck of revenge
eclipsed the bend of my mind.

For years a maggot grew in my belly,
a living coil, white rope bloating like pity.
Self-hatred tacked my body like ticks.
And disappointment took many forms,
mist, a mouse running at my feet.

One morning I saw what I'd allowed
and called for help.

He shot the raven
hooked the maggot
blew disappointment
ripped the ticks
crushed the mouse.

49.

God,
David's your stubborn son.
A freckle-faced rebel,
refusing your outstretched hand
tearing,
        tearing
towards suicide cliffs.

He's a man who savours being *free*.
He's tugged into manhandling wind
that pushes as he gives
you the finger,
calling up to the Sky   'Come on then
                                 Invisible Faker
                                 Come On.'
My boy is hurtling from your hands
            to a brink I can't bridge
            a fall that will rupture
            all   his   milky   bones,
            yes all
            his bones.

And yet, my God, you're young
            like Hercules.
            So   run   Run
faster than predatory wind.
Let your hands unfurl

            as rescue nets
            as rescue nets.

50.

O God of Abraham,
how irrelevant
how embarrassing
how tedious
is your Name in all of Wales.

O God of Isaac,
how offensive
how abstract
how Male
is your bleeding Name.

O God of Jacob,
how unnecessary
how politically incorrect
how un-Radio 4
to mention your Name.

O Elohei Avraham, Yitzchak v'Ya'acov how trivial
how dry the taste
of your name on the tongue.

51.

There are things never to be satisfied:
Self-pity. Hell. Fire.
The both of You.

52.

You're leaving.
Yet if the Advocate had not been
on our side, how much worse
this would all be.

Not yet angry, I look goodbye
into your autumn face, pulling
away into the sodden hills of November.
Rickity-clickity, run, run, run – your body
    leaving my body
along lines of rusty steel.

We argued by the rocks.
Pressed out words we shouldn't.
Teased and trashed each other.
I have drunk bowls of tears.
It could have been floods and seas.

'Don't waste your energy,'
you should have said.

I would have. Yes, I would have
poured myself out without stint
for there are things that make earth ecstatic:
The ways of a man
with a woman.
The ways of a man.

53.

I shouldn't say goddammit,
                    goddammit.

54.

Goddamn computer,
updating old mistakes;
dredging crisscrossed verses
long ago tossed   for good reason
Welcome back!

Goddamn
public printer jamming
my goddamn prayers.

Goddamn you,
David.
You raided my space,
injected yourself.
You are unable to see things calmly
and neither am I.
Goddamn you.

*

What's wrong with my mouth?

Vinegar shot with sugar
cursing, cursing like a crow.

What's wrong with my theology?
I'm liberated,
don't want justice,
        need mercy.

55.

A daily assault clips each turn of thought.
The only escape is unreasonable.
I give thanks to the vanilla wafer saviour
I've chewed, swallowed since turning seven.

With all the words I know but can't say I'll speak.
I'll step into the gritty wind of acclamation
that hurts like sandpaper. My only escape
is to sing without shame.

To show an ecstasy though I cringe Britishly in a queue.
To dance like a Hasidic Jew though I'm Gentile
as Jane Austen. To praise a presence I can't see
for nothing – there's the rub – there's no guarantee
this praise will bring him back to me.
God, you're no genie but a lamp.
Under your light I'll empty the congealed
honey in me.

56.

I hate *no*.
When I beg, plead, reason and still
                              No.

I hate 3am.

That I nearly had the chance,
not once but twice,
and twice again for good measure.

Yes, the meek will choir over the earth,
but what about the disappointed
what's their tune?

I hate uncertainty,
lack of a plan. The skid of my slap-
dash, make-it-up-as-I go
approach. I burn, break, bleed.

Despite all
(perhaps because)

favour comes.

57.

For I am not without The Great Collector of broken things
heeled deep into the ground. Things with missing parts,
kicked-in faces. Things that ought to be binned or burned.

He's that man who walks along the beach
at all possible hours, gathering the wood that lies
like tangled up bones washed up on brittle sand.
Bones in a mesh of blue rope, green cider bottles.

It's always been his way.
He's a gentle one, bigger up close.
He won't be stopped.

I should know.
I was those bones.

58.

We meet my friends; 'church people,'
by which you mean:
'quiche eaters,
side-huggers,
hand-squeezers,
men who wear socks in bed.'

You analyse them across the linen covered table,
they consider you through candlelight.

Over custard and crumble we strayed
into talk of prayers. You snorted,
said it's like a child's bludgeoned knee
kissed better.
I stirred your meaning, squeezing
subtleties like lemon juice
over the peppery sounds of your hot tongue,
as if to say —

59.

As you speak I'm learning
to accept. I chose you, after all,
a Godless psalm-singer,
you chose me, a pale believer.
As knives sharpen knives,
you watch
my mouth.
I gossip
on the phone,
read aloud
the bits from Betty Macdonald
that make me laugh.

I call to you across the way.
Curse you through my teeth.
Your stance gnaws, yet
I face you each day.
I am your map.
Without me you may be lost.
I'd be left unread.

60.

Scent of sweet potato rises.
I turn down the blue
flame, simmering red
onions, renunciations:

I will not demand.
He cannot give.

I dice chicken breast,
red peppers, garlic.

What he cannot change
I'll not demand.

The navy evening air breathes
in
out,
a memory

★

Her shoulder bone,
                lips.

I will not
        demand
                demand

demand.

61.

I remember the day I chose David.
I was a fledgling. Now I am not.

He gathered me in, utterly,
no dithering,   no nit-picking
for chinks   slips   receipts.

He has kept hold of me.
I have kept hold of him.

We slammed the door shut.
Now I am in a universe
spiked with revelation.

62.

David my funny one
offers me plates and plates
of those sugared cakes of unhappiness
I like so much.

God, you are firm with this one;
      I writhe,
        do not know what to do.

Why are you always right
in the long-away end of things?
      Fasten this bird heart
that flaps in your face
nips your fingers.

Defiance is apple-sweet but it's a backpack
too heavy for my shoulders.

              I'm bored of it.
I reach for you,
uncurling the finger of every finger
the eyes within my eyes.
I call from the depth of my throat.
I am a seagull lobbing my body
rough into the wide elements
for you are
life, life, life.

63.

My house is high on rocks.
I was not touched by the flood.
Yet in dreams I see inexplicable waters.
Misplaced streams flow from room
to room like thoughts of another world.
Fountains burst from stone floors, showering
quiet rooms. Condensation trickles the walls
like laughter, glistens on the polished sideboard.
Shafts of rain cascade through the slate
roof thundering around me.
I wade in sunlit rooms, content.
I wake.
Breathe,
scent of beeswax,
water.

64.

Sitting next to the kettle
cross-legged on the counter
we drink Peroni
                    lips pop
                    with each swig
                    dizzy
already!

You cut lacy slices of parmesan, toast
brown bread   spread
too much salted butter.

Everything's ordered:
my round-
bottomed percolator,
packets of couscous,
cannelloni tubes, curry.

Floor's scrubbed,
the essentials tidy
in this breezy shell of a room
where you wiggle to iPod drums.

65.

Please don't stop
me from loving David.
I rest in his freckled arms
that squeeze and bruise
deliciously my transmitter skin.

He will weaken like mint.
His grasp will release.
I cannot trust in him alone.

There are things I can't ignore.
Your ways make pictures
I recognize. The sounds & rhythms
accelerate an answer in me.

I've laced myself into faith.
I'm a lone tree, swaying by a river.
Is David a cloud of chaff
without roots attached to you?

Will this be a stark shaking of hands?

66.

David
you've the integrity of rock,
gentleness,
expanded   this far.

Anymore,   I'll break.

You taste   smell
of home.

Relentlessly glad,
desperate
        in your presence
        I can't stay long.

I've come empty   as
a kiss can be.

67.

David, for once,
speaks in a metaphor,
badly.
Something like
our music's fallen to a minor chord —

his having to leave
— cannot say where
how long.

'Life's a bitch,' he says.
'I'll not leave you pining,
listening to the news all day.

Anything could happen to me.

I'm cutting this thread between us,
letting you flap free.'

68.

So   go
but know
I'm not sending you.

Leave the linked-
up
pattern we've woven

                                        lived in
your fleece, my grey socks.

You've refused
the chance
to become new as a goose egg.

        I'm all cat's shrills

bone-butting iron
throat-thickening fish mouth
soundless.

69.

You should never have kissed me
                    nor I you.
Mouths incite miracle.
Eros is Holy. Yes. Over soap suds,
scalding taps, metal-scour,
our spirits ram; we are head-locked
you yank my boundaries
not elastic bands –
dumb looks blinking,
the horizon of my face,
                    breaking.

Look. My pilgrim hands,
like yours *always* gentle,
empty. They've formed meatballs,
unlocked doors, picked up onion skins
from my kitchen floor.

You've fixed the coffee plunger,
pulled me up the hill,
thumbed tears I wouldn't explain.

We're made of bones like nerve endings
burnt out branches   a white sky.

We're scratched by other's traces,
that thing you deny:
Spirit.

It's not benign,
breaks us in half like a baguette.

70.

Grey birds lift slowly, part to roll
as we come close. I cannot rise
above my feet, held down by earth's
hard hands; on narrow tracks in shoes
not meant for walking far, I walk
this long sea night, pausing
on benches, kicking the iron bar.
Your arm tight over my shoulder
I speak to you of Agape
in disjointed silences,
in looks
in teeth-gritting tears.

If I could ask for one thing
I would
splinter you like rock, drink
your waters that spurt like DNA
beyond generations; drown you
into a white-capped, infinite life
where your heart parts,
lifts as I come close.

71.

Night was an over-turned bowl,
when you arrived.
You were overturned.

You left with the morning star,
when you drove away.
You saw the morning star.

Your face was set like flint,
when you left.
Your face was dry as flint.

Alone in a Mustard Mini,
alone on a shadowy lane.
You moved with the morning star.

Dawn was a bowl of light
when you left,
a bowl of light.

72.

The card says "light a candle
to represent your prayer."
Twenty-pence for a wick,
a flame   a quiet corner.

Let David go
in silence like smoky lavender.

Let your pain melt down
into waxy little stalactites.
Tomorrow morning it will be grated
from the iron rack by the verger.

I don't have time for candles.
Stand back.
Open both the doors.
Clear the Altar.
I'm coming up the aisle
dragging an uprooted oak,
a can of paraffin.

My prayer will burn for days.

73.

Pottery is ferocious.
Squelchy hands thump
me on a wheel.
The potter dips
into my dry-mud
throws   pulls   presses
my pagan sludge.
I am becoming Plate,
Cup   Bowl.

I spin,   spin alone
in a room of fire.
I burn whole.

Here I am,
pulled from smoke

            unbroken.

74.

Steering round roads, flagged by associations
I see pieces of bone
in the hills, woven in grass and stony bristle
along the paths; a jaw
lies open in a stream.
I have been up there before and I'll
go again.
Down here I lift up my eyes to the relics
in the hills, to a tractor
boy grown up, who winced as he flattened
the things around him.
He stood with me in the valley; faced me
in the bracken,
bellowing not for the divine
but for me   his canticle the call
of imagined water.
He was born with suspicion
in his throat, I kinetic with spirit.
Together we traced the borders, trod
the foothills, rolled
the foam flecked waves, the gritty beaches, the salt
cold depths
of his home. He wanted to be a dragon-
tailed warrior.
He spoke in a language I could only
feel. There are bones in the memory
of that boy who shambled off to war,
no forwarding address.
I stayed here
          hovering steep on the brink,
jittery with my own longing, which he pressed into me

a recurring pain searing the dark
tissue,
the marrow, the cells of all
the guts I've got.

My foot would have slipped but the Rescuer
was already there, and knew the whole boring story.
He caught me
like a scent,
a look.

75.

I arrived home empty
needing to be rinsed.

I'm hollowed out

glass jar
emptied,

rinsed.

★

From my bedroom window I watch
the afternoon gigantic

darting machines clatter,
digger dark dinosaurs
clawing
the beach   a yellow sweep
scabbed with clay   lime green weeds,
copper rust
loose coins   rocks.

★

I'm e n g u l f e d
in a white haze of prayers.
God, turn me by the shoulders to face the stripping wind.

★

Frail
my masts, flapping
a gale of blue light   orange fireball
crisis at sea
inside   churning.

★

Every ceramic, clothes, charity shop
is cloying red   purple   gold
incense – superficially sacred –
makes me
sick
sick
sick.

★

In the house of earth, I sense a multitude of hidden spaces;
through a crack in the wall another room like a cave
I can only explore alone.
David can't see.
I cannot force his lids,
his eyes, hard as green marbles.

★

Am I reduced by faith or expanded?
By saying yes to belief, I take in density
like oatmeal; yet I say no to David,
his bulk and human roughage.

★

The song on the radio says:
      get tough or die.
I will draw a line under this grief.

Only choice
grit
your name
makes strong.

76.

I'll get a poem out of you yet, Black Lion, for all your roaring, panting, stalking.
I'll pick it out from the smoke of your mane after the bonfire. I'll grab it
from the rough and tumble in your poke-about finger eyes. The words are loose
and flying
for they live in all you have done and all you won't do
God love you, great Welsh bastard   for I can't.

May blossoms have burst pink, and here you are on the doorstep of my thoughts,
hungry as ever, fat with mistakes I can taste. I remember moving in the shadow of your bulk, a young queen grinning;
the newness of becoming a body that shivers,
an estuary, tugging towards the sea-depth of longing to gather you in, to dissolve
in your rolling warmth for God crafted refuge and love
is a light, a door, a room.

        You thought it a joke inside a cracker.

You saw I was sharp as ice in the morning.
You hovered about; glancing at all I've built.
You were half-tamed, torn between instinct and shame,
knowing if you bit me you must devour the rest and treasure my bones.
I'm not a stray lamb, a dippy bird.
Don't you know how hope deferred made my heart a terrier,
            without shelter,
        an owner,
            only a scrawny poem to chew on?

77.

How deep your aubade pronged
into the throat of my would-be plans.
I believed   (wrongly)
I was designed for your rescue. Desire
cut short still scalds.
We were a skirmish of suggestions,
in the car, kitchen, as you reached to shift
or stir. I stood under your arm.
Now we are separate. I could never be
squashed into your foxhole philosophy.
Mine is a merging; earth and heaven
in grip. Life is a hodgepodge;
a piecing together of bludgeoning glances, cotton-soft
words,
decisions that make me a trooper.
I will hop wider
          you will fall deeper.

78.

Prayers are like pots always on the boil.
I'm stewing in the juices of you.
The garlic scent of your name
stains the kitchen for days.
Let me dry,
traceless to the bone.

I won't talk about you, a waste of energy,
I'll write a poem instead.
I'll forget the very name of you.
Except when I read the Psalms.
David is ever present,
his doubts, his fears.

I won't wish for your safety.
Think of you sweating under canvas
stars, taking orders, deciphering maps.

I'll not decipher you.

79.

The crow that picked the flea
from the back of the pig that ate
the rich earth I ride as tarmac
currents blue, a hidden river between
yellow stubble, harvest dust.
Driving alone with the sun
as a guide; a ripe-hipped woman
making it all happen as it should,
this symbiosis
of breath, step   need. The slow
speed of a day driving by the sea,
nearly home, the bright lived minutes,
blasted by open window air.

The car is packed with brown paper
grocery bags: tomatoes,
a fat cucumber,
seedy brown bread,
daffodils —
a yellow frenetic sadness, my God
reminding me, again:
You shall not be in want.
            Live like that crow.
Take and eat, with joy,
the flea upon the back of the oblivious
pig who gorges on goodness,
            on goodness you *will* live.

80.

My teeth
My teeth
they collapsed,
warm into my cupped palm:
my teeth, a bucket of warm spit,
pink gum-gunk.

Dreams about teeth
      reflect 'anxieties,'
they say. Classically, money, sex, power. Or lack.
                  I rise again.
A snowboarding morning braced
in 'little heels,' trying not to garrotte myself down the hill of tricks,
          slips, turns.
I'm a blue flash, a hip-flexing, head-
ducking, tray-carrying,
quasi-counsellor, teacher
expression reader, prophetess, toilet-
cleaning poet, swerving to avoid rocks,
catch phone calls, meet deadlines,
keep friends,
avoid focaccia bread, not get emotional
or emotionally involved with shits or otherwise.
Keep accurate records, research suicide support networks, not judge
      on a flame
of anger. *Be   real.* Show myself
to the ones I claim. Pray. Read and re-read psalms. Delete the
      spam-mail thoughts
of *endings   catastrophes*
               petty snubs

my throat thickens as I face
a boy with autism, a girl with back problems, bad memories

O this our mouth of falling teeth!

81.

The gardener leans into his spade,
gazing at me as if I were the squashed
earth he tills. He's a known expert.
I chose him to develop this small length of land;
it's all I have. But here I am, asking:
Why, after another year I have a harvest
of only onions   not strawberries,
blueberries   rhubarb.
I've bought the right packets,
left explicit instructions.
The chipped sky shifts and sighs.
He flings my cracked leaves fuming
into a compost of humid days;
coffee grounds, tea bags,
David's love gone dry.
Why so many cuttings here, there?
This constant fertilization's a fire
without flames. This garden's a bristle
of roots that rise, never burst.
Yet I trust this gardener. Our days
are discussions. Circular arguments,
assurances; a period of silence,
another crop of onions.
I search him out, quick in wellies,
raincoat flapping. My jaw set.
He stands still as a seed,
asks that acid question –

'Don't you believe I can finish what I start?'

82.

Yes. Deep still calls to deep
even today as I read Martin Buber on the train.

I must not view the world as *it:*
using all things in relation to my consuming self.
The world is personal,
separate from my own theatre.

> And, as if to illustrate,
> a man and a woman rattle
> longer than the track to Newtown,
> Their voices, loud as a brink
> tripping the flow.

She has three-hundred pounds in her account.
She did the long-distance relationship
thing. She doesn't want him to change
the subject   yet.

> I listen. I read. I can't forget
> him.

How I reared my head, stomped my feet,
galloped headlong into a pile of –

At night I imagine terrible things.

I've stopped reading newspapers.
I won't give up coffee.
I need light at night.
I have tried to keep pure.

Washed my face
in the milky light
that pours each morning
to the floor of my days.

Son of all poets,
where is this baby-like sleep you promised?

83.

I want the biggest blessings
that hang like head-sized
grapes, purple, green.
I saw them as a child
in one of the floods of dreams
I dreamt. I remember lace,
a curtain; outside a nettly English garden,
beyond a brick wall a jungle
of gigantic grapes,
vines thick as ship's rigging.

An owl with penny eyes
clipped on a tree, blinking.
He knew the meaning,
stood guard like a devil.
"Be gone, owl, be gone,"
I whooshed in silence.
"Let me take
what I have been promised."

I woke before I arrived
yet sometimes I wonder,
is this what I am eating now?
My grapes,
these days of purple-
red surprises.

84.

I lie awake; I have become
like a bird alone on a roof.
              I'm a seagull
flapping, caterwauling pleas,
flurried days' jar, yet
today you say I'm the song
of moving feathers.

I mutter as I peck, windy
scraps of life that whirl
about my head. I shit on things.

I'm hungry for the salmon
bagels others chew.
I loom. Tear out binbag innards.
Leave streets bristling
with crunched brown glass,
coupons,
packets of cheese.

              I'm hated;
              trapped
              tricked.

              My legs break
              I drop
into a falling
                    arc.

I plop
at the feet of the bird-creator
who scoops me
                    limitless.

85.

Shine your eyes upon his hunted body.
Watch the fish-like flicker of his thought circles
spread. Speak soft into that space between.

Fuse the copper circuits of his inside chart.
Blood lines of red. Blue veined silence.
Shelter his pliable mind, that sieve, bed
of memory, deep storage cupboard
scrambled dreams.

Pump,
pump,
pump his fiery fist,
home within home,
scooped down, chest-deep.
The slash of light under a door,
spark of movement behind a window.

Hold him, heal him. I cannot
keep him static,
as he is,
alive.

86.

You're in the deserts
I'm reading about, sleeping in caves
where King David hid from Saul.
He whose enemies were by the thousands,

as are yours.

Whose jaws are you shattering like clay?
Whose teeth do you smash?
There's guilt on your back,
on mine.

You said our problems are peanuts
compared to what you've seen.

You are hunted and you hunt.

I'm praying safety will infold you.
Your enemies scattered,
not destroyed.

87.

And David did write.

Wounded.

The letter in my hand
a wilted daffodil,
pungent.

88.

So,
it turns out
I want you,
after all
the fannying about.

Returning to you,
I peel off my suede boots,
drop the keys on the floor with a clang.

Now there is lightness in me.
There is no smugness in your welcome.
No glint of victory.

Your words are direct as a good map.
They go straight to the home of knowing,
the gut,
the heart,
the part that says —

89.

We walk the old walk,
scramble the chilled rocks,
higher
to be alone.
The ground shifts.

It would be wise to go back now.
It would be wise
not to have gone at all.

Listen to sea
the gulls
the old echoes.

David,
your shoulder bone hurts me.

90.

Take me,
an apple, bruised on the ground,
wash off my grit with a cold blast from the kitchen tap.

Pull David up,
a carrot, the gristly tuft of his hair.
Turn him gently, peel the crusty layer.

Lay us on a wooden board.
Our scent is green like First Morning.
With the sharpest knife pare us down,
Divide   open our skins   other to other.
Cut long ways   across;
orange cubes   orange chunks.
Red curls   white slices   spiral
        roll into one pot   throw in salt.

91.

I wake and know,

David's an atheist after God's own heart.

92.

Driving to Bala through March ice.
Goodbye is bloated,
wilting snow.

I count each chilled mile on fingerless gloves.
Salted chocolate melts dark in my pocket.
The clock in the car, always an hour ahead,
ticks and ticks.

David watches the road, ice
and shadow.
He must recover.
I must continue
the shovelling out of days;
the beat and pat of a newly-made path.
The fogged up world hides streams that will thaw.

I'll carry God
David
into my un-shaped days.

93.

Before I die I want to roar
a song that judders
my neighbour's walls,
shakes you, my big-
eared God and stirs
David from his sleep.

I can't play the sax
I can't bang a drum
I can't work the flute
I can't pick the harp
but I can respond.

ACKNOWLEDGMENTS

First, thank you to Matthew Francis, who has been a trustworthy guide during the writing of this collection. Thank you to Tiffany Atkinson for her encouragement to study the Psalms, and feedback on many of these poems.

Thank you to the following poets whose insightful responses to *Psalmody* were so encouraging: Janet McCann, George Hobson, Carrie Etter, Richard Marggraf Turley, Elin Ap Hywel, Elizabeth Cook, Amy McCauley and Katherine Stansfield.

Thank you to Jan Fortune for publishing some of these poems in *Envio* and Cinnamon Press anthologies. Thanks also to the *New Welsh Review*, *Magma*, *Popshot*, and *Scintilla: The Vaughan Association* for publishing poems in this collection.

Thank you to Toby Martinez de las Rivas, to Todd Swift for publishing this collection, and to Kelly Davio for editing it with me, patiently. Finally, thank you to all the Apichella clan: my parents Michael and Judy, and siblings Lizzie, Caroline, Francesca and Mikey.

EYEWEAR PUBLISHING